Community Helpers

Firefighters

by Cari Meister

Bullfrog
Books

Ideas for Parents and Teachers

Bullfrog Books let children practice reading informational text at the earliest reading levels. Repetition, familiar words, and photo labels support early readers.

Before Reading

- **Discuss the cover photo. What does it tell them?**

- **Look at the picture glossary together. Read and discuss the words.**

Read the Book

- **"Walk" through the book and look at the photos. Let the child ask questions. Point out the photo labels.**

- **Read the book to the child, or have him or her read independently.**

After Reading

- **Prompt the child to think more. Ask: Have you ever met a firefighter? What do the fire trucks in your town look like?**

Bullfrog Books are published by Jump!
5357 Penn Avenue South
Minneapolis, MN 55419
www.jumplibrary.com

Library of Congress Cataloging-in-Publication Data
Meister, Cari.
  Firefighters / by Cari Meister.
    pages cm. -- (Bullfrog books. Community helpers)
  Includes bibliographical references and index.
  Summary: "This photo-illustrated book for early readers tells how firefighters fight fires and keep people safe"-- Provided by publisher.
  ISBN 978-1-62031-075-5 (hardcover : alk. paper) -- ISBN 978-1-62496-031-4 (ebook)
  1. Fire extinction--Juvenile literature. 2. Fire fighters--Juvenile literature. I. Title.
  TH9148.M37 2014
  363.37--dc23
                                    2012044149

Series Editor: Rebecca Glaser
Series Designer: Ellen Huber
Book Designer: Danny Nanos

Photo Credits: All photos from Shutterstock except: Alamy, 4, 7, 18; Dreamstime, cover; iStockphoto, 22; Superstock, 17

Printed in the United States of America at Corporate Graphics in North Mankato, Minnesota.

5-2013 / PO 1003
10 9 8 7 6 5 4 3 2 1

Table of Contents

Firefighters at Work

Ava wants to be a firefighter.

What do firefighters do?

They put out fires.

They help people in danger.
They teach kids fire safety.

Here comes a fire truck!

Lights flash.

A siren sounds.

Firefighters pull out a long hose.

They hook it to a hydrant.

Whoosh!

Out comes water.

hydrant

Oh no!

Dan is still in the house.

Ron goes to get him.

mask

Ron has a mask.

He has an air tank.

air tank

They help him breathe.

15

Firefighters wear
special suits.

They keep out heat.

Ron carries an ax.

It breaks the
window.

Ron finds Dan.

Dan is safe.

The firefighters
put out the fire.

Firefighters do good work!

At the Fire Station

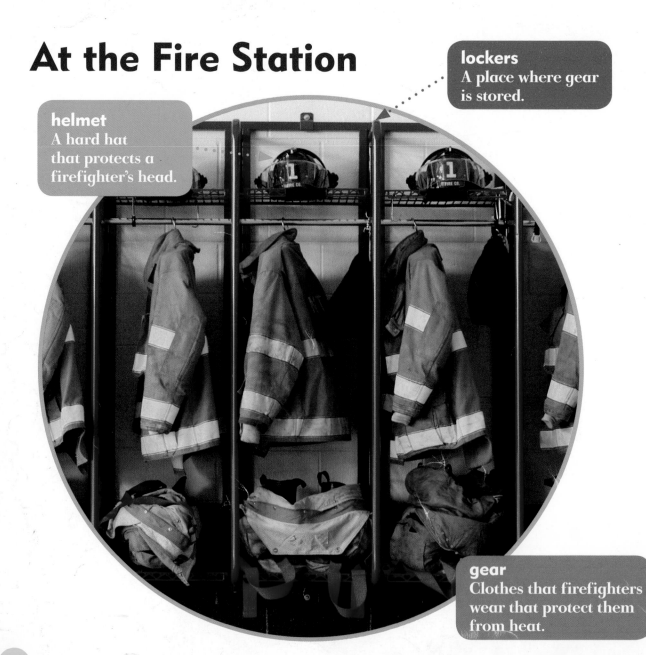

lockers
A place where gear is stored.

helmet
A hard hat that protects a firefighter's head.

gear
Clothes that firefighters wear that protect them from heat.

22

Picture Glossary

air tank
A container that holds clean air for breathing.

hydrant
A big pipe connected to a water supply, for use in emergencies.

ax
A tool with a sharp blade on the end.

mask
A covering for the face; firefighters' masks connect to their air tanks so they can breathe.

hose
A long tube that water travels through.

siren
A thing that makes a loud sound, used to warn people.

Index

To Learn More

Learning more is as easy as 1, 2, 3.

1) Go to www.factsurfer.com

2) Enter "firefighters" into the search box.

3) Click the "Surf" button to see a list of websites.

With factsurfer.com, finding more information is just a click away.